Maria Ferguson is a writer and ⌐
has been a resident artist for th
Arts Centre and commissioned I
Stylist and BBC Radio 1. Her de
Dance, sold out performances a
Saboteur Award for Best Spoken

Essex Girl, was shortlisted for Soho Theatre's Tony Craze Award and won Show of the Week at VAULT Festival 2019. *Alright, Girl?* is her debut poetry collection.

MARIA FERGUSON
ALRIGHT, GIRL?

Karen and Iain,
Thanks for your
support!
I really hope you
enjoy my book.

Maria

Burning Eye

Supported using public funding by

ARTS COUNCIL ENGLAND

This edition published by Burning Eye Books 2020

www.burningeye.co.uk

@burningeyebooks

Burning Eye Books
15 West Hill, Portishead, BS20 6LG

ISBN 978-1-911570-74-5

Printed in the United Kingdom by Imprint Digital

ALRIGHT, GIRL?

For Matt,
who always makes sure I'm alright.

CONTENTS

WHERE EVERYBODY KNEW THE KRAYS

*These toffs! Drink a bottle in our boozer, think that makes 'em
one of us? They don't know anything about this place. What?
With their artisan bread and their coffee shops, they can sod
right off...*

Her words land like chocolate limes
melting on my tongue.
Gold-clad knuckles rapped down on tables,
thick chains, her pub.

They told me of back-room gatherings,
betting slips for fights on the sly,
bare fists. How they'd seen men close to death
or worse before they'd pack it in.

They told me about the ICF
and how they met the Krays.
Have I told you that one, babe?

They never knew family breakfasts,
mahogany wooden tables in kitchens,
fingers sticky with jam turning pages
of the papers, no, love.

It was Rosy Lee from Annette upstairs,
beer mats, affairs, Silk Cut.

I still remember that night
we could have died in Manor Park,
hiding in the chicken shop,
must have been, what, fifteen?

Remember that dry cleaner's on Green Street?
Intercom and tinted windows,
dodgy dealings, stolen watches,
stolen meat from Marks',
Here, darlin', I'll do it for ya cheap.

They gave me advice on bar stools over gin and bitter lemon:

Stay east, my girl, and this side of the river, yeah? Don't you
    go wandering too far. What about your old man?

I say, *He's Belfast born, but Canning Town.*

Good lad... but is he West Ham?

When my mum and dad got married,
they went straight from the church to Upton Park.
Technically their wedding dance was to
'I'm Forever Blowing Bubbles', and my favourite photograph
is of my dad, holding her up in front of the stands.

So, yeah... till he dies, I reply.
Throw in a *Come on, you Irons!* for effect.

Well then, that makes you one of us, sunshine,
and I know you're destined for greater things,
but don't you dare forget it.

When I pulled pints in IG1 there were men
at eight in the morning begging
for their two John Smith's.
They told me about the good old days

in baseball caps, with chicken heads,
in gold-clad knuckles, thick chains,
I'm hard, me, babe. I knew the twins,
you know the twins, the Krays?

They'd drink well into the day,
home for a kip, back by six,
they filled my shifts with stories.

You can 'ave that one for free, treacle,
so long as you write it down.
Make us famous one day, eh?

I told them I would,
I will.

MY SISTER IS FIVE YEARS OLDER THAN ME

It was a hot summer, or at least a hot day,
when we brought water balloons into the garden,
filled them up by the outside tap,
hid behind the little shrubbery we had,
garden furniture, worn-out shed.

We squealed as the cold liquid burst
on our bodies, shook it off like wet dogs.
Maybe she had tired of war.
Maybe she needed the loo.
I just remember her bounding up the stairs,

me by the kitchen, watching their movement.
You can't hide them in your bra! That's cheating!
Her pale skin flushed. Shoulders shivering,
drips on the carpet. It was only then I realised
how much of a woman she is.

BRAVE

They told me I was.
Teachers, friends' parents
in kitchens, girls I grew up with.

I have only ever felt it once.
Laid out naked with the lights on,
showing you where it hurts.

ALRIGHT, MATE?

It's all betting slips and free papers.
Crosswords and quiz shows.
Casual misogyny I let slide,
but only for the ones I like.

The evening creeps closer with each pint;
this is a ritual. Daily dose of weak lager and,
You alright, mate?
Yeah, I'm alright.

Tobacco tins on the bar, prized treasure.
Amber Leaf, filter tips and liquorice Rizla.
They tell old stories with new vigour,
play their parts.

Joker, pisshead, keep myself to myself
and read the paper.
I don't know why I come in here.
Plenty of other places to drink.

Bite your lip.
Sip your pint.
You alright, mate?
Yeah, I'm alright.

One's wife left him for another man.
One never sees his son.
One went bankrupt and disappeared,
couldn't afford his daily habit,
started wasting away, alone at home

but they found him. Nearly broke down the door.
Passed a pint glass round for bread and milk,
brought Tupperware of home-cooked meals.
They put him back on his feet.

Next time I see him his clothes don't fit.
His voice is quieter, eyes darker, hands shaking
as he reaches for a pint someone else had to buy
and all I can manage is,

You alright, mate?
Yeah, I'm alright.

SLEEP

Last night I slept in too many clothes.
Layers of cotton, blankets, feathers;
the heaviness forced me to sleep.

I buy clothes that don't fit.
Men's shirts,
oversized dresses,

drown myself in fabric.
My shape fluctuates too often
for me to make my peace.

My body pretends to be stable;
it thinks I am stupid.
He used to be more careful

when he touched it.
He used to say my name.
I've started to forget what it sounds like.

How the syllables have
the ability to sink into skin
and keep you warm.

How back then,
even naked,
I could sleep.

KIRSTY

I peel my jeans away from my skin. Feel the heat at the top of my legs, a stinging above my belly button, wince, look down. Red... I have a burnt arse... and belly. They told me do six minutes, it's pointless otherwise, and I'd never been on a sunbed before; I thought, *fine*. Rebecca Jones has one in her house, which is probably why she's always the colour of a Hobnob. I'm more Rich Tea at best, and I'm happy with that, usually, but the ball is coming up, or 'prom', as people keep saying because we're American apparently all of a sudden, and we didn't get one in Year 11 'cause they know everyone will get drunk, and all-girls Catholic schools aren't exactly known for their leniency when it comes to lawbreaking or general debauchery, so now I'm eighteen with a sunburnt arse, even though my arse has never seen the sun and probably never will (which isn't true, because of that thing I will do in Australia, but I don't know about that yet), and I've got a dress from Coast that doesn't fit, but it's the biggest they had and it's perfect, apart from the fact that it doesn't fit, but it nearly does, and I have another week to eat nothing but lettuce, and it cost 180 quid, so my mother is livid, which is fair enough, really; she's just paid 180 quid on a dress that doesn't fit, *but it will, it will, I promise it will*, and the water is freezing. I am clutching the wall as it falls on my red belly, which has also never seen the sun, incidentally, but my arms and chest are quite tanned, actually; I might be headed more towards a sort of Malted Milk, and I turn around and my arse is on fire and how could this much sodding damage be done in *six minutes*? But my legs look pretty good too, actually. It's not like anyone's gonna see my arse, or my belly. I'm going with Matt, who doesn't want to shag me but he'll turn up on time, and I'm patting my arse and belly dry now, I've nicked some moisturiser from under the sink and it's cold on the raging furnace that is my arse cheek and I make a sort of involuntary song out of *ha hoo he haha ha* and that dress *will* fit me. And my skin will be the right shade of biscuit. And my make-up will be flawless and my hair will be bleached with just the right amount of peroxide and my nails will be fake, made of acrylic and French manicured and my heels will hurt like fucking hell and give me blisters I won't be able to get rid of for two weeks but they'll make me look taller and slimmer and I will stand in front of a limousine with a corsage on my wrist, next to a boy wearing a suit and a pink tie to match my corsage, and we will link arms and smile so that one day I can look back at that photograph and show it to my kids and say, *Look, darling. That's your mummy!* And they'll think I look young and pretty and thin. They might even think I look happy.

HANNAH

Only an hour out of the smoke
there is a place I can go near the water.
She lives on the top floor, wall of windows.

We walk to the front to see the boats and pubs,
seagulls eating chips. I ask to see the cockle sheds
and we sit on cold stone; it looks like it might rain.

We lived together, not too far away from here,
when we were younger, not as tired,
not as worried about life.

I say I can't believe our age.
That I don't know what else I can do,
what more I have to give.

She asks me the question I have been hoping
someone will ask for months now and I reply.
Throwing my one-word secret

from the pit of my stomach onto the water,
watching it skim the surface,
waiting for it to sink.

ALL THE THINGS I NEVER SAID

I know you're leaving, but what if you stayed?

I feel like a child,
feel like a clock,
like paper.

(I'm not making sense,
this is torture.)

What if I told you it's crying?
Told you it's ticking?
It's blank?

I know you're a child, but what if you stayed?

I feel like a clock,
feel like torture,
like ticking.

(I'm not blank,
this is crying.)

What if I told you it's making sense?
Told you it's leaving?
It's paper?

I know you're ticking, but what if you stayed?

I feel like crying,
feel like a child,
like a clock.

(I'm not leaving,
this is making sense.)

What if I told you it's paper?
Told you it's blank?
It's torture.

BURN

after Ruth Stone

I must leave it uncovered,
feed it air – it scabs and blisters
and I feel embarrassed, cover
with dressings and tape.

People ask, *What have you done?*
I say, *I've been silly.*
It's my fault, really.
I hurt myself.

I walk around knowing
that if it scars, I have only
myself to blame.
I tend to it every night.

Watch the scabs change colour,
escape in the shower.
Leave a strange pink flesh
like a newborn.

TEN

We wear green-and-white checked dresses.
Play off-ground touch and scrape our knees.
We compare our gummy smiles,
count out saved-up compensation
to buy flying saucers and chocolate limes.

We swap food from lunchboxes.
Decide we'll wear the same top to a party,
pretend it's a coincidence.
We are both now obsessed with Dalmatians
and have matching stationery.

We phone each other every day,
even on holiday.
We want to go to the same big school
where our sisters go already,
help each other with SAT revision.

We discuss in great detail the likelihood
of magical creatures' existence.
How the Tooth Fairy and Easter Bunny
are a bit condescending now, actually.
Santa is a maybe. Jesus is definitely real.

MY LETTERS

after Hugo Williams

They are under the bed.
Burning a hole in the carpet again.
I can smell the fabric singe.

Cigarette lit from the hob, eighteen, drunk
on tequila I bought to impress you,
forgot the limes.

Used a Cif synthetic lemon I found in the cupboard
to ease the taste; it's the last thing I remember,
that smell of burning hair.

Some I have kept for almost a decade.
My handwriting has changed a little;
they are tired things and sad.

They long to be held by your fingers,
they want you to understand, but it's been
so long and there are so many now,

these letters I write and do not send.
I think you're meant to throw them away
but I never get that far.

They are hiding under bank statements,
photographs, receipts,
self-destructing, overheating.

I taste it on my tongue, Saxa,
cheap tequila. You sat on my bed
that night, asked me what was burning.

ALRIGHT, LOVE?

I throw away the most precious word
I will ever have to give, to a man
down the pub who points to a pump
and sips his pint in silence.

SMILE

It's the *cheer up* ones.
The *go on, it won't kill you* ones.
The *it might never happen* ones.
The *oh, what's wrong with you?* ones.
The *was it something I said?* ones.
The *you're not very friendly* ones.
The *are you one of them lesbians?* ones.
The *you look so much prettier* ones.
The *I'm only having a laugh* ones.
The *can't you take a joke, babe?* ones.

And maybe I can't, you know?
Maybe I can't.

HALLOWEEN

I wore my big coat last night for the first time this winter. The one I got at that market in Italy even though it was twenty-five degrees. I wanted to spoil myself. Bring back some of whatever had gone to make me feel okay again. I had boot prints on my stomach. Dust in my hair. He said he'd never hurt me. I had a white pizza with seafood. Crisp white wine. I read Armitage by the pool and rose from the dead. I wore my red dress. I went walking. I didn't know you existed yet. He said he would never hurt me. I wear a silver ring most days with a green stone in it. The one I got at that market in Italy. I wanted to spoil myself. It needs a clean. I had sex with you this morning. Last night I cried twice. You made me tea and jam on toast. I've made it out alive. I mention his name in your company. I don't know why. He said he would never hurt me. My jeans were getting tight. What took us so long? Why didn't you realise? The boys are all on acid. They're listening to Elton John. I wanted so badly to be loved. We've put the heating on. Nearly November. Nearly twenty-nine. Nearly telling you how I feel. From this position I can only see one of your eyes. I keep mine open sometimes when we kiss. I think you might like my body. It makes me not hate it so much. It is colder but the sun is out. Crisp white wine. He said he would never hurt me. Sticky strawberry jam. Let's share this slice. Orange juice. Another train. I need a new pair of trainers. My hair is getting long. I might throw out his books. This isn't the poem I wanted to write. Different vinyl every week. MDMA on a DVD. Throwing up acid and cider. I kiss you everywhere. There's a woman on the train looking at me like she knows exactly what I am thinking. I look away and she smiles. Nearly twenty-nine. I almost say it this time. I mouth it to your back. He said he would never hurt me. I couldn't get out of bed. Not even to shower. Not even to piss. Another UTI. This jam's got whole strawberries in it. Sticky lips. You tie me to the bed. He said he would never hurt me. 'Rocket Man' on repeat. I try to find you in the dark. I've never been good at explaining myself. I say things without thinking. Let me think. Sinking into your sofa. Châteauneuf-du-Pape. He said he would never, never, never. It's all a bit scary, isn't it? We stay in bed till two. Boot prints on my stomach. Your smile in the mornings. Dust in my hair. If he did you wouldn't know it. If he did you wouldn't know it, darling, would you? Would you know it?

FIFTEEN

I meet you at the hairdresser's,
you've just had your highlights done.
You are wearing jeans and a tight pink top.
I am wearing navy trackies and a baby blue hoodie.

We somehow acquire alcohol.
Big bottles of alcopops, WKD and Smirnoff Ice.
We are going to meet some boys who called me fat.
The one I hate is going out with one of your lot.

We have different friendship circles now.
We're still best mates but we've changed.
We go under the subway with the booze.
The police come and we leg it.

I stop once we've lost them and down the bottle.
Massive glugs of fizzy, fruity liquid.
It bubbles in my belly, then rises to my throat.
I retch and it comes easily, a constant stream of blue.

YORK ROAD

We were the scum of the earth, us.
Limescale bath and we loved it.
Didn't you share one once?
With Jonny. At a party.

In that house where we grew into ourselves,
pushed each other to limits we didn't know we had.
Early bacon sandwiches when none of us had slept.

We danced with shadows we threw
against walls that moved quickly, involuntarily.
You said you saw a spaceship
where the lampshade should have been.

Went to the shop in your socks.
Sang yourself to silence in a corner,
came back hours later with a jolt.
The best one yet, you said.

That night Mike gave me a piggyback
because I couldn't walk or see
and our eyes were flying saucers
and my limbs were melted wax.

I don't remember any of the things I think I should.
Where you grew up. How you took your tea.
I just remember the feeling of being infinite.
I'm the scum of the earth, me.

THREE YEARS

I'm sorry, mate.
I forgot the date.
I had be reminded
by Facebook.

A page dedicated only to days
like this, or your birthday,
or how it buckles our knees
on a Tuesday morning.

A photo found in a box
or drawer, parasols in a field
and eyes that hadn't closed
for two nights.

We made our memories out of powder
on mirrors and cheap wine.
Clung on to each other in the 6ams
when reality hit.

I haven't visited that place in a while.
I'm getting old.

I remember at your funeral
someone said you will always
be young and beautiful.
It seems a high price to pay.

In the station, where we met that day,
me in a skirt I thought was too short,
we had a whisky for you
while we waited for the train
and I knew then I'd lost him for good.

He hasn't been the same since you left.
Three years and so much has changed.
I barely speak to some of them now.

Those boys I rested my weight upon
in the nights that we didn't sleep.

You held us together, I think.
You hold us together, I think.

RUNNING WATER

You always said you could never understand
why people would leave the water
running when they brush their teeth.
That it's such a waste of water.
It's such a waste.

I am a wasteful person.
I buy food I don't eat,
make tea I rarely finish,
rip out page after page after page,
spend money that isn't mine.

But if I'm brushing my teeth
and I realise the water's running
I turn it off immediately,
say *sorry* to an empty room.
It is in this moment

I remember you most vividly.
How quickly you were taken.
How we shook our heads
in disbelief. How we said,
It's such a waste.

COMMON

I called myself it in public once,
something of a defence mechanism,
and this woman in her (probably) forties,
wearing a lot of expensive-looking jewellery,
told me not to use *that word*.
I think she was offended. Poor her.

TWENTY

We talk on the phone for the first time in weeks.
You're in your second year at university
and I just started drama school.
You ask me if there are a lot of people singing on tables
and I say yes, because there are.

You have a handful of contact hours a week
and a nightclub on campus. I am in school
every day, from nine to six, mainly screaming at trees.
We are both drinking most days
and fancy people we shouldn't fancy.

You say I should come visit soon.
There's a big night coming up with fancy dress.
You've learned how to make Skittle vodka
and the train's not very expensive.
We decide we will both go as mimes.

I'm jealous of your new friends; they sound nice.
I miss you, but I don't know how to tell you that.
I'm worried that I still haven't had a proper boyfriend,
but I don't tell you that either.
Before you hang up you tell me to stop smoking.

BODY

Body is problematic.
Body is hungry but scared of eating.
Body is beautiful
only when somebody says that it is,
but body is living.

Body is singing itself to sleep
on a cold night in February.
Body is giving a speech
to a room full of people
with spinach in its teeth.

Body is dancing to great music
in an awful club
and sweating
and not giving a fuck.

Body is trying on all the clothes
it bought from ASOS
and giving a front room catwalk
to the cat.

Body is getting bigger,
and smaller, and bigger
again, but body is
starting to accept that.

Body will eat in public now.
Body will have sex with the lights on.
Body will try on jeans in a shop changing room
and won't take it too personally if they don't fit.

If body doesn't fit into old clothes
it buys new ones;
it doesn't shrink.

Body is trying very hard to be well.
Body is going to the gym, sometimes,
if it feels like it.
Body is moisturising every night
and enjoying the feel of itself.

Body is starting to think
that it might be possible to fall in love
with another body, but only when
body is beautiful without somebody
saying it is.

PRIMROSE HILL

You showed me the whole of London and I wanted to eat it all,
so I snapped off the tops of the buildings like breadsticks
and made them a part of me.

I ate all the pods on the Eye, those lions in Trafalgar Square
and the river and Tower Bridge.

The view went on for miles, a buffet at an expensive wedding.
The belly of St Paul's shaking with fear in the haze of an August sky.

My mouth opened and closed several times and you thought I
was lost for words but I was trying to swallow it up: the roof of
the pub and the buses and the dogs and the foxes.

I ate a man in a suit and tie on his way home to his wife and a girl in
wellington boots.

It is only now, button popped off my jeans and forcing my zip
with a hanger, it occurs to me that, actually, I may have gone too far.

ALRIGHT, GIRL?

It's the call of the blokes I know
from trading notes for pints of John Smith's.
The relief of another living,
breathing thing in an empty pub in January.

It's a longing for a lost wife, or three,
a smile as their palm is graced with change,
they hold on a little too long.

It's the raise of the hand or curt nod
when I see them in the street
away from beer mats and tired stories,
tired eyes, rosy cheeks.

A greeting in a familiar kitchen, the same
questions to follow each time:
How's the poetry?
How's the love life?

It's the cabbie who knows the East End
like the freckles on his wife's nose.
Rolls out names that might impress.
Jack the Hat. Billy the Bomb.

It's the barman on a Saturday night when I said
I'd only have one, and my eyes are red and my mouth
is dry and all I really want is his voice to be

my dad's on the end of the line, miles away,
killing time, with that question I never know
the answer to.

THINGS I AM SCARED OF

Spiders
Breaking bones
The people I love dying
Masks
Putting on weight
Murderers and rapists
Donald Trump
Not having kids and regretting it
Having kids and regretting it
Failing
Falling
Guns

TWENTY-FIVE

I call you on a Saturday morning.
I haven't been to bed.
It is summer and the sun is shining
in someone else's garden.

It's your birthday, and you've gone away
with your boyfriend.
I am still wearing last night's dress.
Drinking cider from a champagne flute.

He's asked you to marry him.
My legs nearly give way.
I ask a dozen questions,
tears streaming down my cheeks.

We agree we'll meet up soon
and you'll tell me everything.
I put down the phone, go back inside.
The others are playing Jenga.

They have socks on their hands
and penises drawn on their faces in eyeliner.
I go and get into bed with two sleeping bodies.
I don't know what it means, to be in love.

MIRACLE

after Jameson Fitzpatrick

I woke up and it was a miracle.
I had nowhere to be, but I got out
of bed, and that, in itself, was a miracle.

The tea I made was a miracle,
and how I left you sleeping
because you looked so peaceful,

and the clothes on the floor,
and the wine still in the bottle,
that was definitely a miracle.

The cat purring was a miracle.
The noise from the builders next door,
butter melting on white toast,

the toast on my tongue was a miracle.
I dressed in front of the mirror
and it was a miracle.

I took time to look at myself.
Ran my fingers over my body,
my face, my hair, and thought

it was beautiful.
I smiled, and it was a miracle
to see myself smile back.

THESE PANTS COST THIRTY QUID

Nude and tight. From thigh to breasts
they hold in new flesh. A year without counting,
of saying yes. Walking instead of running.

I like the way they make me into the shape I was
when Mum was happy and I was not,
and it was all too easy to find someone who wanted me.

We drink gin and tonic in your front room.
You tell me that the Stones were better than the Beatles
and I tell you exactly why you are wrong.

It is only when you push me down onto my back,
shoes still on and wrapped around your body,
dress inching further up my leg, I remember.

Nude and tight. From thigh to breasts,
holding in flesh, progress.
The parts of me I've gained.

In the morning I sit on the edge of the bed
wearing only my dress.
Drooping breasts and round belly visible

beneath the fabric,
and your head, resting on my lap,
as if in worship.

QUESTIONS

Can you pay your rent?
Do you need some help?
How you getting on?
Are you feeling better?
Have you found a job?
Have you seen my shoes?
Shall we do this again?
Could you pass me that?
Are you eating?
Do you have to go?
What time should we meet?
Do you love me?
Are you crazy?
Did you see your mum?
Have you lost weight?
Have you brushed your teeth?
Can I go first?
Are you hungry?
Does that feel good?
Do you like that?
Am I hurting you?
Is it worth it?
Are you tired?
Are you okay?
Did you mean what you said?
Are you happy now?
Sorry, what was the question?

TRYING

I still don't like myself every day,
but you do, so I'm trying to.

On the rare occasion you wake before me
I open my eyes to the face of a child
who has finally got that special thing
at the top of their Christmas list.

I am the Nintendo 64,
PS3, Tamagotchi.
I am the thing
that didn't come easy.

You are a long-awaited holiday,
a cold beer at the end of a long shift,
a text back from my brother,
a bloody miracle.

It has been dry for thirty-one days straight
and our bodies stick to the sheets.
In the mornings I reach for you like the water
we keep on our bedside table. I swallow you whole.

There are still days I want
to cover all the mirrors.
Try on every piece of clothing I own,
decide to stay at home.

It is on these days, like any other,
you tell me I am beautiful.
Pick out a dress you like: *Try this one.*
See, look. That's nice.

One of these days the sky will break.
The rain will fall, and I will dance in it.
I will dance in it with you.

I may not like myself every day,
but because of you I'm trying to.
Because of you, I'm trying.

THIRTY

We sit in a café near your house
down the road from our old school.
Your little one is sleeping
and we are drinking coffee.

We have diamonds on our ring fingers.
Life is hard and we are happy.
She wakes, confused and grumpy,
so we take her to the park.

We pass the public toilets
where I took my first pregnancy test.
We push her on the swings,
point to things of interest.

Speak in one-word sentences.
Doggy!
Slide!
Ball!

You look at her with love I can't yet comprehend.
I am proud of everything that's led us here.
There are still monsters hiding underneath our beds,
though you'll swear blind to her they don't exist.

I DON'T KNOW WHY I LIVE IN LONDON

Every penny I earn is spent
before it lands in my bank.
Every landlord fixing on the cheap –

paint and plaster over old fittings,
old pipes, boiler on the blink,
multiple jumpers over central heating.

I have looked at the gas meter
eight times this week
and my frown lines are getting deeper.

I've forgotten I'm in love.
That it shouldn't matter if the water's gone cold
and we're boiling kettles to wash up.

TO GLASGOW

In that city far away enough to warrant
first-class we feel like high-fliers.
Get change from fivers for our pints,
Might as well stay for another.

Free hot pies at closing time.
Songs and dancing and strangers
smoking in doorways beckoning us in.

He took me here on our first trip away,
three days in December. We barely left the flat
before dark, drank mulled wine at a winter market,
Buckfast at the Necropolis.

My body swelled closer to him,
desperate to be touched.
Ripened like fruit in his hands.

I gave myself completely in that bed
that creaked like the night.
Held his hand on a cobbled street,
a late-night dinner, then *one more drink.*

We scaled the length and breadth of that city
as the wind picked up and the rain froze
and not once, not once did I feel the cold.

GARGOYLES

Now that you love me my clothes don't fit.
I sit with you and drink red wine.
I barely look in the mirror.
Sometimes, the guilt creeps in; you kiss it out of me.
You tell me how much you love my body.
I believe you every time.

I didn't think I'd have the time
to find the perfect fit.
Spent so many years hating my body.
Numbed myself with wine.
There were gargoyles living inside me,
pulling faces in the mirror.

You check your rear-view mirror.
We finally have some time.
You don't dare look at me.
One eye off the road and you'd have a fit.
Back seat clinking with bottles of wine.
I am desperate for your body.

Are you desperate for mine? My body?
I stand naked; you become my mirror.
This used to take a bottle of wine.
Undressing used to slow down time.
Not knowing if I was the right fit,
it put the fear of God in me.

Never felt natural to me,
sharing my naked body,
worried it would never fit
a man's desire, gargoyles in the mirror.
But with you I take my time.
Savour it like an expensive wine.

We sit and drink red wine.
It soothes every part of me.
It's moving quickly now, the time.

It's taking its toll on my body.
You stand with me in front of the mirror,
your arms around my waist, the perfect fit.

There will be endless glasses of wine, a constantly changing body.
Gargoyles always inside me, showing themselves in the mirror.
I will make my peace with the cruel hands of time, now that I have
    found somewhere, someone that I fit.

ALRIGHT, SON?

Been coming here since he was a baby.
Only sees his dad at weekends,
so Sundays are spent in the pub.
Pound in for a game of corners
whenever the footy's on.

He listens to music, plays on his phone.
Rolls his eyes from the sidelines,
listening to the lads' banter.
Two quid for a bag of sweets.
Glass after glass of Pepsi.

They all know his name.
Pat him on the back, ruffle his hair.
I've watched him grow from behind this ramp.
Seventeen, he is now, and never even a cheeky half.
Except for his grandad's funeral:

Free pass today, mate,
just make sure you have a few Scotch eggs.

He kept it together.
Blamed the red eyes on his pint.
Blinked back the tears with nods and sniffs
as every bloke gave the same advice:
Chin up, son. You're alright.

PUB QUIZ

Eight thirty every Sunday.
Our pub, where it all started.
Three-pound pints and Fat Les
on the jukie. Roger behind the bar.

For weeks you say all you want
is for him to remember our order,
so when he takes my mini-prosecco
out of the fridge without asking
your face lights up like a Christmas tree.

This is it, you say.
We've made it.

First-name terms with Neil, our quizmaster.
This is his living, his pride and joy.
Writing rounds on general knowledge,
sport, music, entertainment.
We pray for Robbie Williams.
He gives us Beatrix Potter.

We groan or cheer at the table round,
World Cup winners or past PMs.
We stroke our chins, use bookies' pens.
Say things like,

Come on, I know this one!
I'll kick myself if it's wrong!

Taking more chances with each empty glass,
months of coming second-last.
Half-time blues, the chocolate round,
blaming it on the size of our team.

We've done well for just you and me, babe.
Look over there, there's loads of them!
Of course they're gonna bloody win!

We despair at our mistakes, revel in
our victories, say things like,
'Course it is! I should have bloody got that!
That's what I said!

Or *sorry.*
Just *sorry.*

We jeer if the bar team win,
It's a fix, it's a bloody fix!
Pat each other on the back
if we somehow manage to place.
Treat the prize of a bottle of wine
like a BAFTA.

Win or lose, there is a stack
of pound coins on the table,
and we play our songs till closing time,
wrap tighter around each other.
Then at kick-out time we leave together.

Say, *Cheers, Rog.*
See you next week

HIPS

You've always been sturdy, wide.
Ironically named child-bearing.
You'd make it easier, apparently.
The moans and heavy breathing.
The pushing and the pain.

You've been different lately, though.
Softer round the edges.
Aching when the bleeding comes
or when the little girl on the bus
reaches for my sleeve.

SONNET FOR MY GIRLS

I have seen the chunks of vomit in their hair.
The make-up smudged across their pasty cheeks.
We've taken turns in playing Truth or Dare,
Had arguments that carry on for weeks.
I've danced with them till dawn in dingy clubs.
We've waited for the bus with cheesy chips.
They've given me their shoes when mine have rubbed,
Then forced sambuca shots upon my lips.
They've taken all my hurt into their hearts.
I've seen them become mothers, become wives.
We've laughed the pain away before it starts,
Then held each other's hand when it arrives.
Still, I don't think these women know their worth.
Or how they are the centre of my earth.

CHANGES

I work in a pub where the men
remember *their* East End.
Nods of the head from flat caps,
camel coats and dogs.

Where they found solace in betting shops,
and Sundays meant church and roast beef.
Where women were sets of keys, necessities
in back pockets, and Green Street was sacred.

With fear in their eyes
and gravel voices they say,
It's not the same.
It's changing.

The kids all buy fried chicken. Eat it on the bus
with smatterings of ketchup and burger sauce.
They remind them of a lost perfume.
A language they don't speak.

I tell them about my nan,
cockney through and through.
Used to drape over her balcony
to watch West Ham.

Insisted on pie and mash and liquor.
Go on, try a jellied eel.
She was whisky and brooches and curls.
Cigarettes and sovereigns.

Proper East End I am, my girl.
Declared with pride
from the back of her throat.
Proper East End, she said.

I have seen how hard it is to be a part
of this furniture. It can make a young man

old. But it settles in your skin,
to the marrow of your bones.

So when I sit in the pub with the men
who pay my rent, I listen carefully.
Feed on words over gin and tonic,
the things we share, my heritage.

And when they tell me it is changing
I say, *I am changing with it.*

ACKNOWLEDGEMENTS

My thanks to the editors and staff at the following publications where earlier versions of some of these poems appeared: *The Dizziness of Freedom* (Bad Betty Press, 2018), *Stepney Words III* (Apples and Snakes, 2017).

Parts of the poem 'Kirsty' appear in my play *Essex Girl*, published by Oberon Books (2019).

Thanks to all at Burning Eye, especially Bridget Hart, for their advice and support.

Thanks to Suzi Corker for the beautiful cover photo and to Clive Birnie for the design.

Thanks to all the facilitators whose wonderful workshops inspired drafts of some of these poems, including Caroline Bird, Ben Norris, Andrew McMillan and Helen Mort.

Thanks to Amy Acre and Toby Campion for helping me figure it all out.

Thanks to Salena Godden and Joelle Taylor for their kind words.

Thanks to Ceira and all at the Blakesley Arms, as well as the regulars of the Great Spoon of Ilford and Ye Olde Black Bull, Stratford. You have inspired me endlessly.

Thanks to Steph for allowing me to write about our wonderful friendship. Long may it continue.

Thanks to my girls. You know who you are.

Thanks to the ones who hurt me.

Thanks to the Fergs for their unwavering support.

Thanks to Nanny Cis, I wish you were here to read this, and to see your balcony on the front of a book.

Finally, thanks to Matt for believing in me, even when I don't believe in myself. I would not have been able to do this without the miracle of your love.